FUN FACT FILE:
ANIMAL
ADAPTATIONS

20 FUN FACTS ABOUT INSECT ADAPTATIONS

By Kristen Rajczak

Gareth Stevens
PUBLISHING

Please visit our website, www.garethstevens.com. For a free color catalog of all our high-quality books, call toll free 1-800-542-2595 or fax 1-877-542-2596.

Library of Congress Cataloging-in-Publication Data

Rajczak, Kristen, author.
 20 fun facts about insect adaptations / Kristen Rajczak.
    pages cm. — (Fun fact file. Animal adaptations)
 Includes bibliographical references index.
 ISBN 978-1-4824-4449-0 (pbk.)
 ISBN 978-1-4824-4393-6 (6 pack)
 ISBN 978-1-4824-4431-5 (library binding)
 1. Insects—Miscellanea—Juvenile literature. 2. Adaptation (Biology)—Juvenile literature. 3. Children's questions and answers. I. Title. II. Title: Twenty fun facts about insect adaptations. III. Title: Insect adaptations.
 QL467.2.R343 2016
 595.702—dc23
                                            2015021628

First Edition

Published in 2017 by
Gareth Stevens Publishing
111 East 14th Street, Suite 349
New York, NY 10003

Copyright © 2017 Gareth Stevens Publishing

Designer: Andrea Davison-Bartolotta
Editor: Kristen Nelson

Photo credits: Cover, p. 1 James Laurie/Shutterstock.com; p. 4 irin-k/Shutterstock.com; p. 5 Andrey Pavlov/Shutterstock.com; p. 6 DEA Picture Library/Getty Images; p. 7 Thomas Ames Jr./Getty Images; p. 8 Tim Graham/Getty Images; p. 9 Marek Velechovsky/Shutterstock.com; p. 10 Eric Isselee/Shutterstock.com; p. 11 (top left) PlotPhoto/Shutterstock.com; p. 11 (top right) Wally Stemberger/Shutterstock.com; pp. 11 (middle left), 12 Katarina Christenson/Shutterstock.com; p. 11 (middle right) Nathanael Siders/Shutterstock.com; p. 11 (bottom left) Barnaby Chambers/Shutterstock.com; p. 11 (bottom right) Phil Jenkins/Shutterstock.com; p. 13 Lovelyday12/iStock/Thinkstock; p. 14 Adegsm/Getty Images; p. 15 Brian Lasenby/Shutterstock.com; p. 16 cosmin/iStock/Thinkstock; p. 17 Norrabhudit/iStock/Thinkstock; p. 18 Andrew Skolnick/Shutterstock.com; p. 19 Jasper_Lensselink_Photography/Shutterstock.com; p. 20 Vitalii Hulai/Shutterstock.com; p. 21 (top) Marcel Jancovic/Shutterstock.com; p. 21 (bottom) xpixel/Shutterstock.com; pp. 22, 23 (butterflies) Sari ONeal/Shutterstock.com; p. 23 (stamp) johavel/iStock/Thinkstock; p. 24 Nature's Images/Getty Images; p. 25 natbits/iStock/Thinkstock; p. 26 (top) Inventori/iStock/Thinkstock; p. 26 (bottom) defun/iStock/Thinkstock; p. 27 Klaus Kaulitzki/Shutterstock.com; p. 28 Stephen Bonk/iStock/Thinkstock; p. 29 Photo Researchers/Getty Images.

Printed in the United States of America

CPSIA compliance information: Batch #CS16GS: For further information contact Gareth Stevens, New York, New York at 1-800-542-2595.

Contents

Words in the glossary appear in **bold** type the first time they are used in the text.

Millions of Insects

Insects live on every major landmass in every kind of **habitat** around the world. There are about 1 million species, or kinds, of insects, and they come in about as many shapes, sizes, and colors as you can imagine!

Insects as we know them today began to appear around 400 million years ago. Since then, they've **developed** body and

behavioral adaptations, or changes that allow them to move, eat, and survive more easily in their habitat.

All insects have three main body parts, jointed legs, and a hard outer covering called an exoskeleton.

5

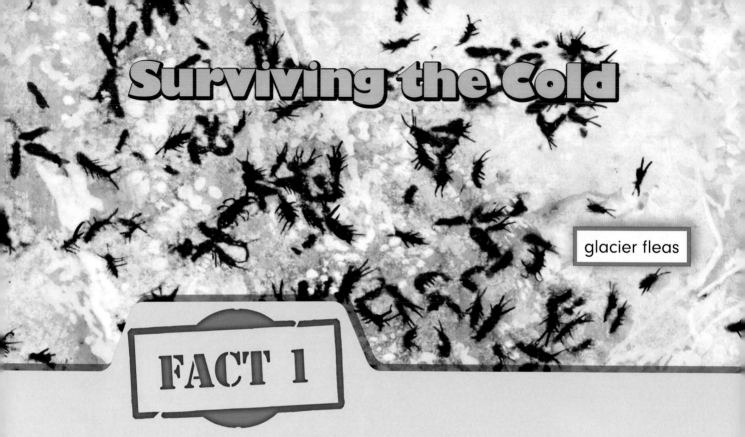

Surviving the Cold

glacier fleas

FACT 1

Many insects survive in the Arctic by using homemade antifreeze.

Some species of insects are able to live in cold places because their body makes cryoprotectants. This matter keeps their body safe during freezing. Springtails survived being frozen for 4 years in one study!

When it's too cold, some insects stop growing, eating, and moving around.

Diapause is the period when an insect's body shuts down for a time because outside conditions could harm the insect. Diapause often happens during winter for insects that live in a place with four seasons.

The Arctic is home to more than 1,000 kinds of insects, including caddis flies.

FACT 3

Honeybees bunch together in a tight ball to stay warm.

Below 64°F (17.7°C), honeybees need to warm up! In the middle of the ball, bees **vibrate** their wings to make heat. The bees on the outside hold the heat in. Almost all the bees take a turn on the colder outside—except the queen. She stays in the ball's center, nice and warm!

Honeybees have other behaviors that are adaptations. They learn how to collect honey and **pollinate** flowers from other honeybees!

midge

Some midges build special cocoons for winter.

Midges make cocoons in summer, but their winter cocoons are stronger. They're built very close to midge larvae bodies. Scientists believe the cocoons **protect** the midges from harm that could be caused by water freezing around them.

FACT 5

Insect mouthparts have developed to be perfect for what each kind likes to eat.

Insects, such as crickets, that eat plants or other insects have mouthparts for chewing. Butterflies and other insects that drink plant nectar have mouthparts they use like a straw!

Houseflies have sponging mouthparts. They throw up on their food so it's soft enough for them to sponge up.

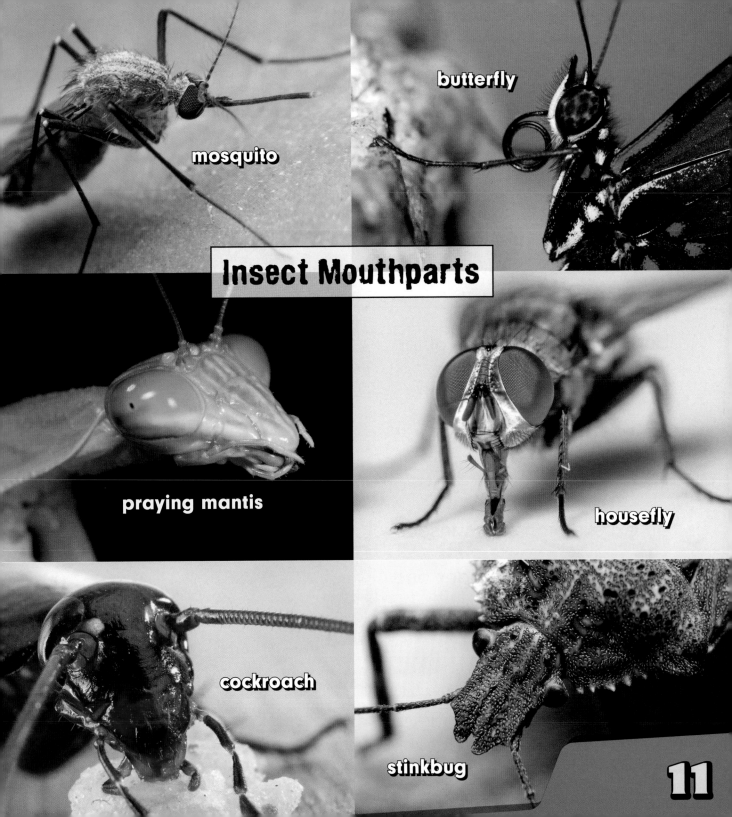

Insect Mouthparts

mosquito

butterfly

praying mantis

housefly

cockroach

stinkbug

11

When insects outgrow their exoskeleton, they get rid of it.

Insects have a soft body inside their hard outer covering. This exoskeleton can't get bigger as the insect body does. The loss of an exoskeleton so an insect can grow a new, bigger one is called molting.

Insects may molt many times in their life, especially when they're developing into an adult.

An insect's eye size and antennae length have to do with their home and habits.

If an insect lives in a dark place, its eyes are small and its antennae are longer. Their eyes aren't as helpful in the dark! Dragonflies, who live outdoors and are active during the day, have large eyes and small antennae.

Hiding in Plain Sight

FACT 8

The orchid mantis has legs shaped like flower petals.

To people, the orchid mantis looks like the flower it's named for. Scientists think it adapted its body over time to look like a flower to hide from **prey**. It might be able to draw prey in, too.

Can you find the orchid mantis? The way its body is shaped and colored is **camouflage**!

Stick insects sway in the wind, just like the tree parts they're pretending to be.

Stick insects, or walkingsticks, look like parts of plants and trees. They've developed this amazing camouflage to hide from predators. But if they're caught, they can also drop their leg off to escape!

Perfect Proportions

FACT 10

A flea's body allows it to run between the hairs on an animal's body.

Fleas have a body that's flat on its sides. They don't have wings and have short antennae to keep them from getting stuck on animal hairs and fur.

Fleas' mouthparts are tiny so the animals they bite can barely feel them feeding!

Cockroaches' long, thin legs allow them to run really fast.

Insects with long, thin legs often need to run fast to get away from predators. Similarly, grasshoppers' back legs are long and strong for a certain purpose. They're for jumping over tall grass.

Adapt to the Habitat

FACT 12

Aquatic insects sometimes have claws, hooks, and suckers instead of legs and other body parts.

Developing body parts to catch food and move better in water is important for aquatic insects. Giant water bugs have front legs that can grab prey and back legs that are strong for swimming.

giant water bug

Dung beetles eat, lay eggs in, or simply live on animal waste.

Dung beetles have many adaptations for their interesting habitat! Special spikes on their back legs help dung beetles roll dung, or waste, into little balls to lay eggs in or eat. Their front legs are strong for digging into a pile of dung.

Dung beetle antennae aid beetles in finding just the right pile of dung!

Young dragonflies that live in water are called naiads or nymphs.

FACT 14

Young dragonflies live underwater—and have gills for breathing!

Dragonflies lay their eggs in the water. Baby dragonflies live in the water until they're adults. Once they take to the air, young dragonflies have developed enough that they don't need gills anymore.

Mole crickets have front legs specially shaped for shoveling.

Insects that live underground, like the mole cricket, often have body-part adaptations that help them dig. The special shape of the mole cricket's legs allows it to make tunnels in its soil home.

FACT 16

Viceroy butterflies may have adapted to look like the monarch butterfly.

The colors of the monarch butterfly show predators that it's going to taste bad to them. For a long time, scientists thought viceroy butterflies adapted to mimic, or copy, the monarch. It turns out, the viceroy might taste as bad as a monarch to birds!

Brightly colored insects are often poisonous. This makes it easier for predators to remember what not to eat in the future.

pipevine swallowtail

Tell the Difference

MONARCH

wingspan 2 ½ to 3 ⅜ inches (6.3 to 8.6 cm)

- flies to warm places for winter
- caterpillars are black and yellow
- found in North American, South America, the Caribbean, parts of Europe, and Australia

VICEROY

wingspan 3 ⅜ to 4 ⅞ inches (8.6 to 12.4 cm)

- **overwinters** as a caterpillar
- caterpillars are green and brown
- found only in North America

black line across the back wings

The monarch and viceroy look very similar, but have one major difference you can spot!

Poison, Sting, and Stink

FACT 17

The most poisonous caterpillar in the United States is named for its catlike fur.

The puss caterpillar isn't warm and fuzzy! Instead, its fur has **venomous** hairs that can cause a lot of pain. If you ever see one of these—don't touch it!

Venom is an adaptation insects use against animals that might do them harm.

Red fire ants sting multiple times, moving in a circle until they fall off or their victim dies.

Before it stings, a red fire ant gets hold of its victim by biting it. The venomous sting causes a burning feeling and ugly red bumps on a person's skin.

FACT 19

When a honeybee stings a thick-skinned animal, it's killing itself.

Honeybees' stingers have lots of little hooks on them. After a honeybee stings, the stinger can get stuck in an animal's skin—and often rips away the back end of the bee. The honeybee will fly away, but it won't get very far.

Stinkbugs live up to their name.

Stinkbugs give off an unpleasant odor when they feel scared. Scientists believe it may be to warn predators to stay away. Some stinkbugs can spray their smell several inches!

If you see one of these stinkbugs in your house—don't crush it! That just causes them to smell.

Find More Adaptations

From the Arctic to the rainforest, insects have found ways to live in places all over the world. Much of that is due to their incredible adaptations!

There are so many more cool insect adaptations to discover. Army ants can move in waves of thousands of ants, eating whatever is in their path. Some types of wasps lay their eggs inside caterpillars. People may think these adaptations are creepy, but insects are just trying to survive!

wasp eggs growing on caterpillar

Wasps that lay their eggs inside caterpillars have a special body part called an ovipositor used for just this purpose.

aquatic: having to do with the water

behavioral: having to do with the way an animal acts

camouflage: the colors and shapes on an animal that help it blend in with its surroundings

develop: to grow and change over time

gill: the body part that ocean animals such as fish use to breathe in water

habitat: the natural place where an animal or plant lives

overwinter: to survive the winter

petal: one of the soft, colorful parts of a flower

pollinate: to take pollen from one flower, plant, or tree to another

prey: an animal that is hunted by other animals for food

protect: to keep safe

venomous: able to produce a liquid called venom that is harmful to other animals

vibrate: to move back and forth with short, quick movements

For More Information

Books

Boothroyd, Jennifer. *Insect Pollinators.* Minneapolis, MN: Lerner Publications, 2015.

Rooney, Anne. *You Wouldn't Want to Live Without Insects!* New York, NY: Franklin Watts, 2015.

Schuh, Mari. *The World's Biggest Insects.* Minneapolis, MN: Jump!, Inc., 2016.

Websites

Bug Facts: Insects
www.bugfacts.net/insects.php
Read about many kinds of insects.

Bugs (Insects and Arachnids)
www.ducksters.com/animals/bugs.php
Find out all about what makes an insect an insect!

Index